THINK LIKE A SCIENTIST

How to Observe, Experiment and Discover

Written by Susan Martineau

Designed and illustrated by
Vicky Barker

ORCA BOOK PUBLISHERS

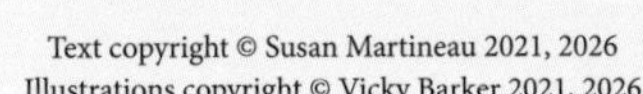

Published in Canada and the United States in 2026 by Orca Book Publishers.

Library and Archives Canada Cataloguing in Publication
Title: Think like a scientist : how to observe, experiment and discover / written by Susan Martineau ; designed and illustrated by Vicky Barker.
Names: Martineau, Susan, author. | Barker, Vicky (Illustrator), illustrator.
Description: Series statement: Question everything ; 2 | Includes index. | Previously published under title: Think like a scientist!: ask questions! read! understand!
Identifiers: Canadiana (print) 20250158124 | Canadiana (ebook) 20250159554 | ISBN 9781459843738 (hardcover) | ISBN 9781459843752 (EPUB) | ISBN 9781459843745 (PDF)
Subjects: LCSH: Science—Juvenile literature. | LCSH: Science—Methodology—Juvenile literature. | LCSH: Science—Terminology—Juvenile literature. | LCSH: Scientists—Juvenile literature.
Classification: LCC Q163.M373 2026 | DDC j500—dc23

Library of Congress Control Number: 2025933022

Summary: This nonfiction book for middle-grade readers shares tips, facts and ideas about how to approach and understand the world from a scientific perspective.

Orca Book Publishers is committed to reducing the consumption of non-renewable resources in the production of our books. We make every effort to use materials that support a sustainable future.

Orca Book Publishers gratefully acknowledges the support for its publishing programs provided by the following agencies: the Government of Canada, the Canada Council for the Arts and the Province of British Columbia through the BC Arts Council and the Book Publishing Tax Credit.

Cover design by Troy Cunningham.
Illustrations and interior design by Vicky Barker.
Edited by Gabrielle Prendergast.

Printed and bound in South Korea.

29 28 27 26 • 1 2 3 4

CERTIFIED CANADIAN PUBLISHER

ORCA BOOK PUBLISHERS
orcabook.com

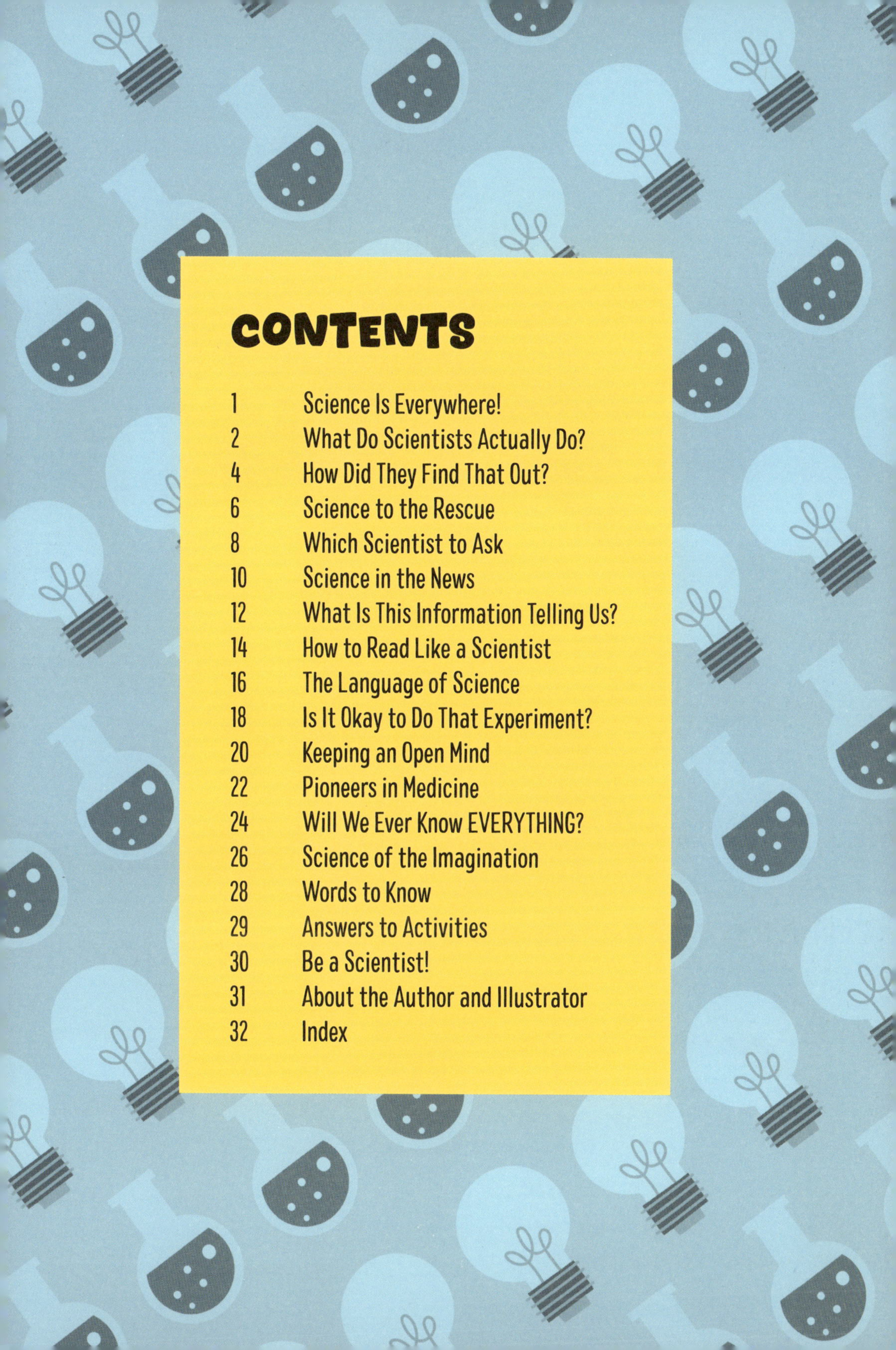

CONTENTS

What is a black hole in space?

Where will there be another earthquake?

What lives in the deepest depths of the oceans?

Do trees talk to each other?

How many lemurs are left in the wild?

Scientists are never finished with their work. They are always finding out new things, and they do this by asking lots of questions, experimenting, observing and then asking more questions.

ACTIVITY

Think about some science news that has intrigued, excited or perhaps worried you recently. Make a list of the questions you want to ask to find out more about it.

WORD TO KNOW

EVIDENCE is anything that helps prove that something is or is not true.

SCIENCE IS EVERYWHERE!

Science helps us find out about everything around us on our beautiful planet and beyond into the universe. It also helps us live safe and healthy lives.

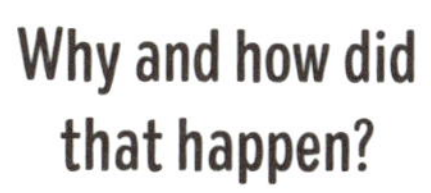

When did it happen?

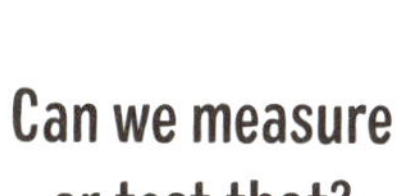

Will it happen again?

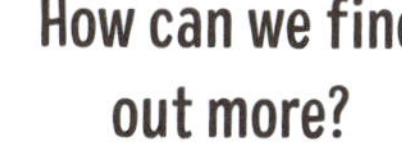

What is that made of?

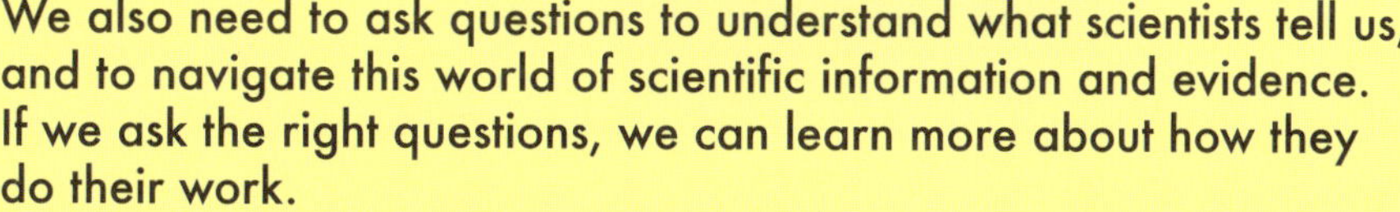

We also need to ask questions to understand what scientists tell us, and to navigate this world of scientific information and evidence. If we ask the right questions, we can learn more about how they do their work.

Asking questions is the best way to find out true facts. There is always more to find out, so maybe you will become a scientist yourself!

WHAT DO SCIENTISTS ACTUALLY DO?

Scientists are like explorers, finding out about the world and everything in it. They ask lots of questions, but how do they find out the answers?

Scientists come up with a possible answer to their question. This is called a...

HYPOTHESIS.

It does not matter if it is right or wrong. It is something they can now **TEST**.

Scientists **TEST** the hypothesis by doing experiments, measuring or observing things. They might even have to make new equipment especially for their experiment.

Scientists look at their results and **EVALUATE** them.

The results might or might not back up the hypothesis. They often end up with even more questions and need to do more experiments!

DESIGN YOUR OWN EXPERIMENT OR TRY THIS EGGSPERIMENT!

The question
What could make an egg float?

The hypothesis
If I add salt to warm water, an egg will float in it.

Equipment *(or apparatus)*

Two large clear jars, two uncooked eggs, a tablespoon for measuring, lots of salt

Method

Fill both jars with very warm water from the tap.
Gently lower an egg into each one.
Then stir several spoonfuls of salt into one jar.

Observe and note what happens!

What conclusions can you draw from the results?
What happens if you repeat the experiment?
How would you improve or change the way you did this activity if you were to do it again?

(See page 29 for an eggsplanation.)

?!?

WAS IT A FAIR TEST?

A test is fair when only one thing is changed (called the independent **variable**) during an experiment and everything else is kept the same. In this experiment, the variable is the salt being added to just one jar. The water and egg are the same in both jars.

WORDS TO KNOW

EVALUATE means to weigh or judge the results of an experiment.

A **CONCLUSION** is what you decide is true after looking carefully at all the evidence or results.

HOW DID THEY FIND THAT OUT?

Do you ever wonder just how scientists have worked out some of the most amazing and interesting animal facts we read about?

How speedy is a cheetah?

Cheetahs have been timed running at amazing speeds in zoos, but what about in the wild?

Scientists attached special tracking collars to five cheetahs in Botswana, Africa. They tracked the animals for 17 months and carefully worked through all the data they collected. They discovered that when the cheetahs were hunting, they accelerated faster than most cars, going from zero to 60 mph (96 kph) in just three seconds!

How many lemurs are left in the wild?

Many species of lemur are in danger of extinction because the forests they live in are being cut or burned down. But can scientists actually work out how many are left in the wild?

Lemurs live in the remote areas of Madagascar and are really hard to spot. Scientists had the clever idea of also counting the trees that lemurs like to eat. They made a "tree map" using the data they had collected. This helped them **estimate** how many lemurs there were in different parts of the forest. This showed people how protecting the trees also helps the lemurs.

Can crows use tools to get fast food?

Crows have been spotted in the wild using sticks to dig bugs out of tree bark, but just how clever are they?

Scientists set up a nifty test for eight Caledonian crows in a laboratory. They did not train them beforehand. The crows were shown a box with a tasty snack in it, along with some bits of stick and thin tubes. All the birds worked out how to put the sticks and tubes together to make a tool for poking the food out of the box!

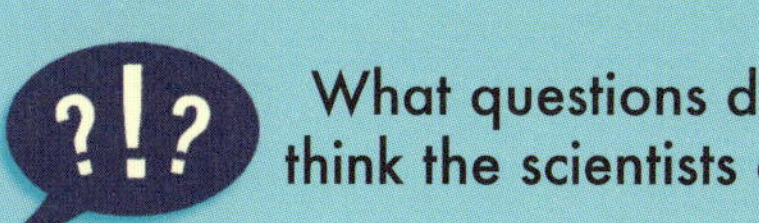

What questions do you think the scientists asked?

HOW CAN WE DO THIS?

CREATIVE PLANNING

OBSERVATION (LOTS!)

RECORDING DATA

CHECKING AND ANALYZING DATA

WHAT DOES THIS INFORMATION TELL US?

They also needed **DETERMINATION** when clambering through a Madagascan forest!

WORDS TO KNOW

DATA is a collection of facts or information, like measurements, numbers or observations. It is a Latin word, and when used in science, it is plural. You say, "The data show," not "the data shows."

ANALYZE means to look at or study something in detail to understand or find out what it means.

?!?

Some birds hop and some walk when they are on the ground. How would you plan an experiment to observe and record this behavior? How would you analyze your data to identify which birds hop and which ones walk?

SCIENCE TO THE RESCUE

When there is a natural disaster, such as an earthquake or volcanic eruption, scientists use their scientific knowledge and skills to become disaster detectives. It is like doing an experiment backward, because they can already see the results.

Why did the ground shake?

What caused that eruption?

Why was there a tsunami?

SAVING LIVES

If scientists can understand why a disaster has happened, they might be able to predict if, when and where another might happen. They can also help people who live in danger zones prepare for the future and become more resilient.

Earthquake-resistant buildings

Flood defenses

Early-warning systems for tsunamis

Seismologists are scientists who study earthquakes. They track and measure the movements of the giant slabs of rock that make up Earth's surface.

Volcanologists study volcanoes. They try to predict when and how volcanoes will erupt.

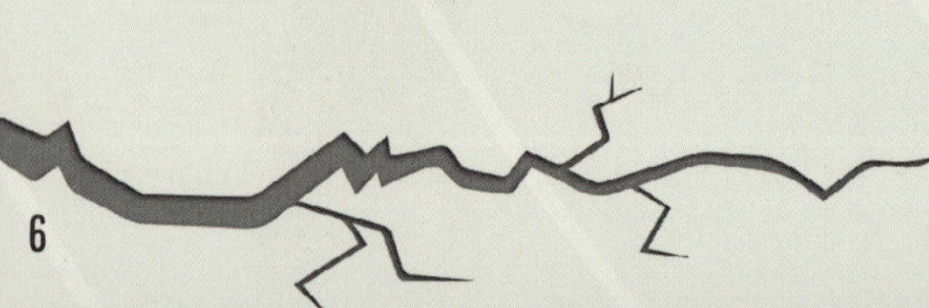

THE MYSTERIOUS EXPLODING LAKE

August 21, 1986
Over 1,700 people died near Lake Nyos in Cameroon, Africa.

WHAT DID THE SCIENTISTS DISCOVER?

The lake is in an old volcanic crater. Carbon dioxide (CO²) builds up at the bottom of the lake.

CAN THEY PREVENT ANOTHER SIMILAR DISASTER?

Teams of scientists have put special tubes in the lake to release the gas and stop such deadly amounts of it building up again.

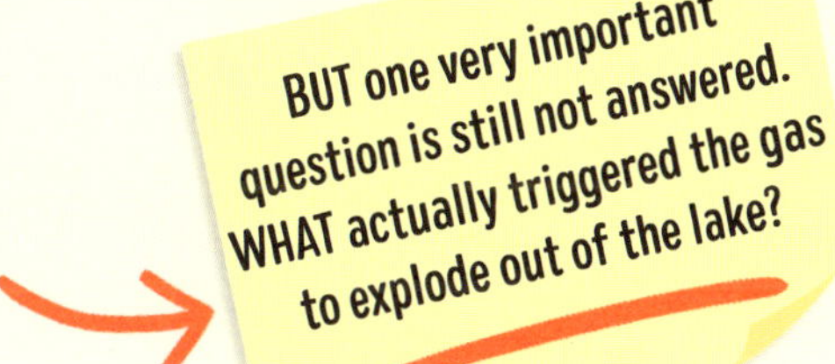

ACTIVITY

You could investigate the science behind another disaster you have read or heard about. What caused the disaster, and might it be prevented from happening again? Is there anything we still don't understand about it yet?

WORDS TO KNOW

RESILIENT means able to survive difficult conditions or recover quickly after a disaster.

CARBON DIOXIDE is the gas we breathe out. It is in the atmosphere around us. Normal amounts of it will not harm you.

WHICH SCIENTIST TO ASK

There are so many different kinds of scientific work that there is probably a scientist working right now on some of the questions you might want to ask and the facts you would like to know.

ACTIVITY

Can you match the scientist to these questions? (Answers on page 29.)
You could think of some other questions and find out which scientist might know the answers. You might want to consult more than one, because scientists also often work together.

A. Ornithologist
B. Astronomer
C. Epidemiologist
D. Oceanographer
E. Paleontologist

(Can you say that out loud?)

1. What is a black hole in space?

2. How much plastic garbage is there in the sea?

SCIENTISTS DON'T ALWAYS AGREE

Scientists sometimes come up with different theories, or ideas, to explain results or evidence.

About 1.2 billion years ago, a massive meteorite smashed down in Scotland, but the geologists (rock scientists) who have investigated this don't agree on exactly where it landed. It might have been where the sea is now, or in a place called Lairg. In Lairg the pull of gravity is slightly weaker than elsewhere. This kind of difference can be the result of a meteorite impact.

In theory, the schoolchildren of Lairg can jump a tiny bit higher than their friends down the road!

WORDS TO KNOW

GRAVITY is the force that pulls everything on Earth toward the center of the planet.

A **BLACK HOLE** is a celestial object that forms after a star has exploded. It has such strong gravity that it sucks light into itself and also disturbs the flow of time, making it slow down near the hole.

SCIENCE IN THE NEWS

Science stories pop up in the news every day. They can make us feel excited, scared or curious. What questions do we need to ask to find out the true facts of the science behind the headlines?

TORNADO TERROR Forecast!

DOGS CAN READ OUR MINDS!

?!?

WHO is writing or sharing this news?

WHERE did they get this information?

WHAT is the scientific evidence behind the story?

- Is it old or new information?
- How do we know if it is fake or not-quite-true news?

TESTS REVEAL LEFT-HANDED PEOPLE ARE SMARTER!

CHILDREN BORN TODAY WILL LIVE UNTIL THEY ARE 100!!!

BEWARE OF THE SHARE!

Science stories are often shared on social media. But the information might not be true or might tell only part of the story. The person writing it might not understand the information or may even have deliberately misrepresented it. Perhaps they are only picking out the bits that agree with what they already believe or want to say.

?!? How would you feel if you were a scientist who had discovered something really amazing only to have it shared inaccurately by other people?

GET THE FACTS STRAIGHT!

ACTIVITY

Find a science story in the news and compare the way it is presented across several news sources. You could then research and verify the science behind the story to find out the facts for yourself. See page 30 for more on how to do this.

WORDS TO KNOW

VERIFY means to check that something is true or correct.

MISREPRESENT means to twist information so that people do not get the true facts.

WHAT IS THIS INFORMATION TELLING US?

Some scientists carry out experiments in the form of studies or surveys. They might be testing a new medicine, researching insects in a particular habitat or seeing if people can tell the difference between real meat and meat they have made in a laboratory.

They end up with a lot of numbers and information to crunch through.

They have to analyze it all and work out what it means.

What connections and patterns can they see?

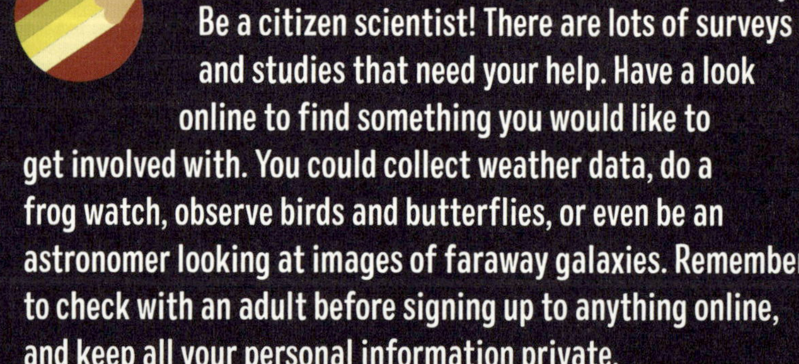

ACTIVITY

Be a citizen scientist! There are lots of surveys and studies that need your help. Have a look online to find something you would like to get involved with. You could collect weather data, do a frog watch, observe birds and butterflies, or even be an astronomer looking at images of faraway galaxies. Remember to check with an adult before signing up to anything online, and keep all your personal information private.

THERE ARE SOME IMPORTANT QUESTIONS TO ASK ABOUT ANY STUDY OR SURVEY.

HOW BIG WAS IT?

How many people took part? How big an area was surveyed? The bigger the study, the more reliable the results will usually be.

HOW QUICKLY WAS IT DONE?

Scientists may be under pressure to find results. Any early news about results will probably not be the final word. More research and studies may be needed to validate their work.

WHO CARRIED IT OUT?

Were they specialists in the area of the study? Did several scientists all work together? Perhaps a series of surveys was done across the world so that they could compare results?

WHO PAID FOR IT?

Was it an independent study? For example, if a burger survey was paid for by the company making the burgers, this needs to be made clear.

BUT always remember that it is really important for any researcher or scientist **NOT** to assume they know what the answers will be before they have done their research.

WORDS TO KNOW

RELIABLE describes information or people you can believe or trust.

VALIDATE means to confirm or prove that something is accurate and true.

HOW TO READ LIKE A SCIENTIST

Scientific information is often shown using infographics like graphs, charts and tables. They should be clear and easy to understand, but it still takes practice to "read" them.

Hopefully these infographics are not confusing at all! Can you understand what they are trying to show? You could try reading them out loud.

How far does the snail travel in a day?

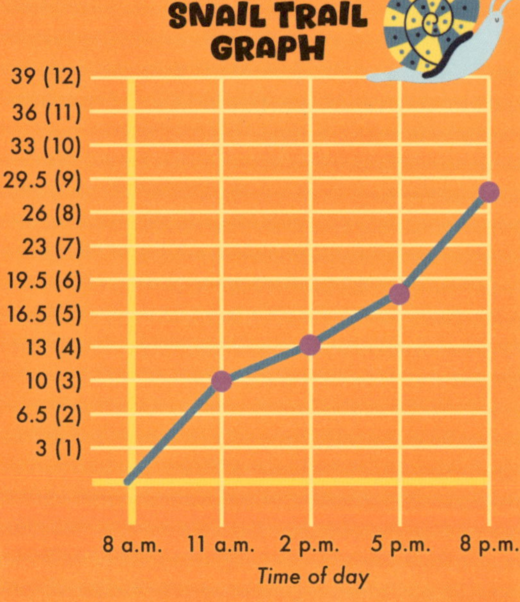

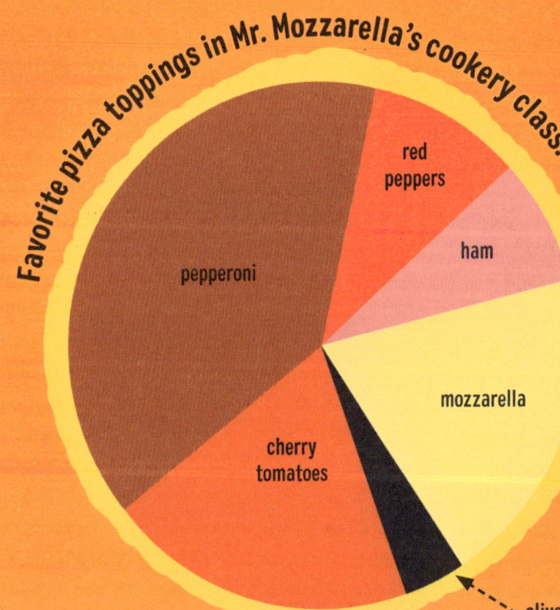

This pie chart is showing me that the most popular topping is pepperoni...and the least favorite is olives.

Thinking is hard work!

The brain uses 20 percent (one-fifth) of your energy, which is quite a lot for a small part of your body!

Don't rush!

Reading and looking at information needs to be done carefully. Do some slow thinking instead of quickly assuming you know what it is telling you. It is worth taking your time to understand something.

Line graphs are a great way to show changes that happen over time. Can you show the following information so that it is clear to anyone reading it? Or you could make up your own graph using data you have gathered yourself.

- At the beginning of week one, the puppy was born. It weighed 10.5 ounces (300 grams).
- By week two it weighed 21 ounces (600 grams).
- For the next three weeks it put on 14 ounces (400 grams) each week.

(See page 29 for a puppy-weight line graph.)

WORD TO KNOW

INFOGRAPHICS are a way of showing information using pictures as well as words and numbers.

THE LANGUAGE OF SCIENCE

Scientists write about their work and display their results using a language that other scientists can understand. They can then repeat experiments or compare results. As soon as we start learning science at school, we are learning the language too!

Using standard units of measurement is really important.

Inches, feet, miles
Millimeters, centimeters, meters, kilometers

height/length/distance

Newtons

force

Degrees Fahrenheit (°F) / degrees Celsius (°C)

temperature

How do measurements relate to each other?
Scientists use handy formulas to show how measurements relate to each other. Here's one for working out the average speed of something:

s = d/t

s means speed
d means distance traveled
t means time taken

The average speed equals the distance traveled divided by the time taken. Nifty and easy to remember! It is why we talk about speed as miles or kilometers per hour.

Distance = 12.5 miles (20 kilometers)

Time = 2 hours

A light-year is a measurement of distance.

It is how far light travels in a year.

1 light-year is about 5.9 trillion miles (9.5 trillion kilometers). The light of the sun takes only 8 minutes to reach Earth, so imagine how far it goes in a year!

1 TRILLION = a million millions = 1 with 12 zeros after it!

Is there a scientific name for everything?
Every known living thing on Earth is named following rules that every scientist across the world follows. It is a system that was started in the eighteenth century when Latin and Greek were the international languages of science.

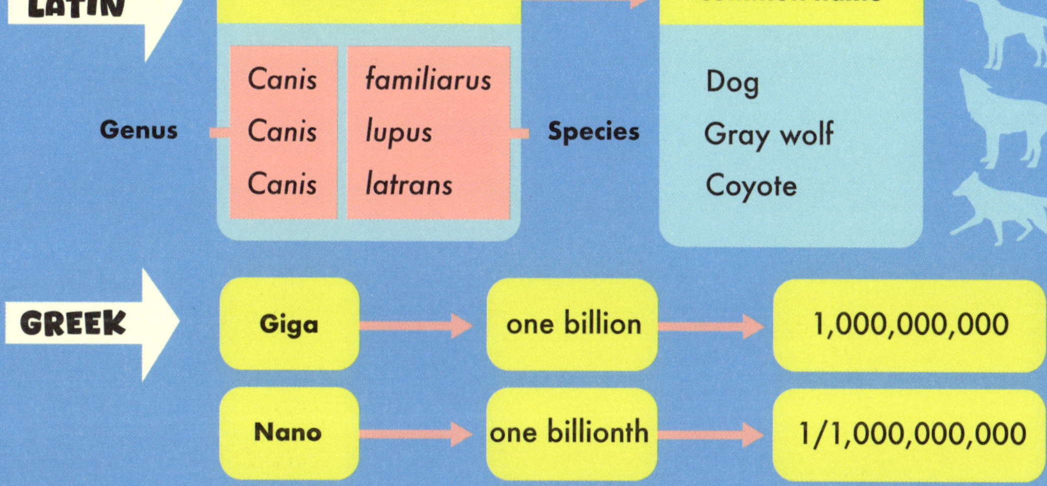

This is helpful shorthand for when there are so many zeros.

ACTIVITY

Can you work out the speed of the bicycle in miles and kilometers per hour?
(See the answer on page 29.)

WORD TO KNOW

A **FORMULA** is a way of showing or working out how pieces of information like measurements relate to each other. Sometimes **FORMULAE** is used as the plural, but **FORMULAS** is more common.

IS IT OKAY TO DO THAT EXPERIMENT?

Whatever scientists are working on, it is important for them, and us, to ask if their experiments will cause any harm. This is sometimes a very difficult question to answer.

Famously risky but amazingly effective!
In 1796 Edward Jenner, an English doctor, carried out a dangerous experiment. He took some cowpox germs and inserted them into the arms of several children, including his own baby son. Then he deliberately infected them with a dreadful disease called smallpox!

The cowpox germs stopped the children from getting smallpox, which was similar to cowpox but much more deadly. We can thank Jenner for this medical breakthrough that he called **vaccination**. But his experiment would never be allowed today. It was unethical.

Vacca is the Latin word for "cow."

Why was it unethical?
Jenner's experiment could have badly harmed the children, if not actually killed them! They certainly had no idea of the danger they were in and had not agreed to take such a risk.

What about experiments on animals?
These are carried out to develop new drugs and test the safety of other products like cosmetics. But is it ethical? Can it ever be all right to hurt animals, even if it means scientists find a new and amazing medicine?

Is it worse to **DO** these experiments than **NOT DO** them and possibly harm humans by not finding this medicine?

ACTIVITY

You could have a debate with your friends or family on the following questions, or you could conduct a survey of friends and family to see if they answer yes or no to them. Write up a consent form for them to sign to say that they are happy to take part in this survey.

1. Do you think it is ever all right to conduct experiments on animals?

2. Would you volunteer for a research program testing a new drug?

WORDS TO KNOW

UNETHICAL describes someone or something that breaks the proper safe and responsible rules of scientific work.

CONSENT means agreement or permission to do something.

CONSENT FORM FOR SURVEY VOLUNTEERS

All information and answers will remain confidential.

I confirm that I am taking part voluntarily in this survey and understand that I may withdraw at any time.

FULL NAME: ____________________

SIGNATURE: ____________________

DATE: ____________________

KEEPING AN OPEN MIND

Sometimes scientists find something completely unexpected during their work, or their results inspire a new invention. This is another reason why scientists need to keep asking questions all the time.

Why did that happen when I did not predict it?

What is the connection between these results?

Have I found something world-changing?

Smart dust
In 2003 a chemistry student called Jamie Link was experimenting with tiny silicon chips when one of them burst into even tinier pieces. She was amazed to discover that they could still work as minuscule sensors.

Not just any old mold!
Bacteria are tiny organisms. Some of them can make us ill. In 1928 Alexander Fleming observed something unusual when he was experimenting with bacteria. One of his samples accidentally ended up with mold on it, and Fleming saw that bacteria did not grow near it. The mold was penicillin, an **antibiotic** that many of us have taken to treat bacterial infections.

The unsquishable bug!
The diabolical ironclad beetle can survive being run over by a car. That is like being crushed by 39,000 times its own weight. Researchers 3D-scanned it at the same time as they tried to squash it. Thankfully, it was not harmed! The beetle's wing cases have interlocking, jigsaw-like pieces that make it superhero tough. Scientists can now develop similar ways of joining different materials, like plastic and metal, to make aircraft or buildings much stronger.

Weird weather
The catastrophic volcanic eruption of Krakatoa in 1883 caused extreme changes in the world's weather and skies. Meteorologists realized that volcanic ash was traveling around Earth high up in the atmosphere. They had discovered the jet stream, a band of very strong winds that whooshes around our planet, several kilometers up in the atmosphere.

Science in space
The International Space Station (ISS) is a laboratory in orbit around our planet. Many of the experiments are designed to find out if humans could ever really live in space and travel farther into the universe.

WORD TO KNOW

A **SILICON CHIP** is a tiny piece of silicon inside a computer. It contains electronic circuits and can store lots of information and do complicated calculations.

ACTIVITY

You can track and spot the ISS in the night sky as it travels overhead. Just download one of the ISS-spotting apps to find out when it will pass near you.

PIONEERS IN MEDICINE

We often read about amazing medical advances, like new vaccines and treatments. But how can we be sure they are safe? What questions do scientists ask to make sure?

What is a vaccine?
A vaccine makes the body's own immune system produce antibodies that can fight off germs that cause disease. It is especially important for diseases caused by **viruses**, because these cannot be treated with antibiotics (see below). Vaccines save millions of lives.

How do they make sure a vaccine is safe?

Testing on animals.

Does it work in the laboratory?

Testing on a small group of up to 100 humans.

All the humans are VOLUNTEERS.

Is it safe for humans? Does it work? Are there any **side effects**?

Testing on several hundred humans.

How do human immune systems react to the vaccine? Are there any side effects?

Viruses are smaller than bacteria. They cause diseases like chickenpox and COVID-19. They cannot be treated with antibiotics.

WORDS TO KNOW

An **ANTIBODY** is a substance that our bodies can make. Antibodies travel in our blood and destroy other substances that carry illnesses.

ERADICATE means to get rid of completely.

Killer disease
In 1967 the deadly disease smallpox killed two million people. By 1979 the disease had been eradicated by worldwide vaccination.

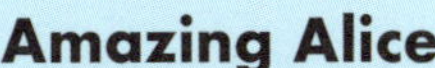

Amazing Alice
Alice Ball was a chemistry professor at the University of Hawaii. In 1916 she discovered a new way to treat people suffering from a terrible skin disease called leprosy. This transformed their lives. Sadly, she died at a young age and was not recognized for her pioneering work for many decades.

Testing on thousands of humans.

They are either given the vaccine or a placebo (something that has no medical effect) to compare results between them.

Are there any rare side effects we haven't spotted yet? How well does the vaccine work on this much larger group of people?

Independent organizations in charge of making sure vaccines and medicines are safe doublecheck the scientists' results. They decide if it is safe to offer the vaccine to everyone.

ACTIVITY

How much do you know about how your body works every day? Do you know where your heart, lungs, liver and stomach are located? Can you find out the names of the parts of your digestive system and track the path of your breakfast through your body?
(See page 29 for answers.)

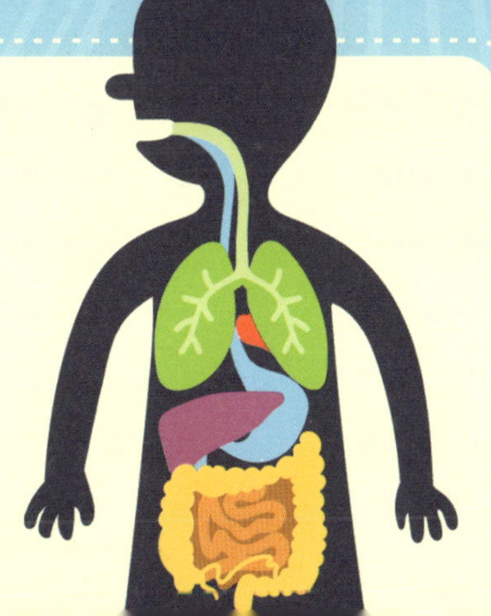

WILL WE EVER KNOW EVERYTHING?

The short answer to this question is no! And the more we know, the more we know we don't know! Even things that we think we know now could change as scientists carry on their work.

We all need to keep asking questions too. But most of us have done that since we learned to talk!

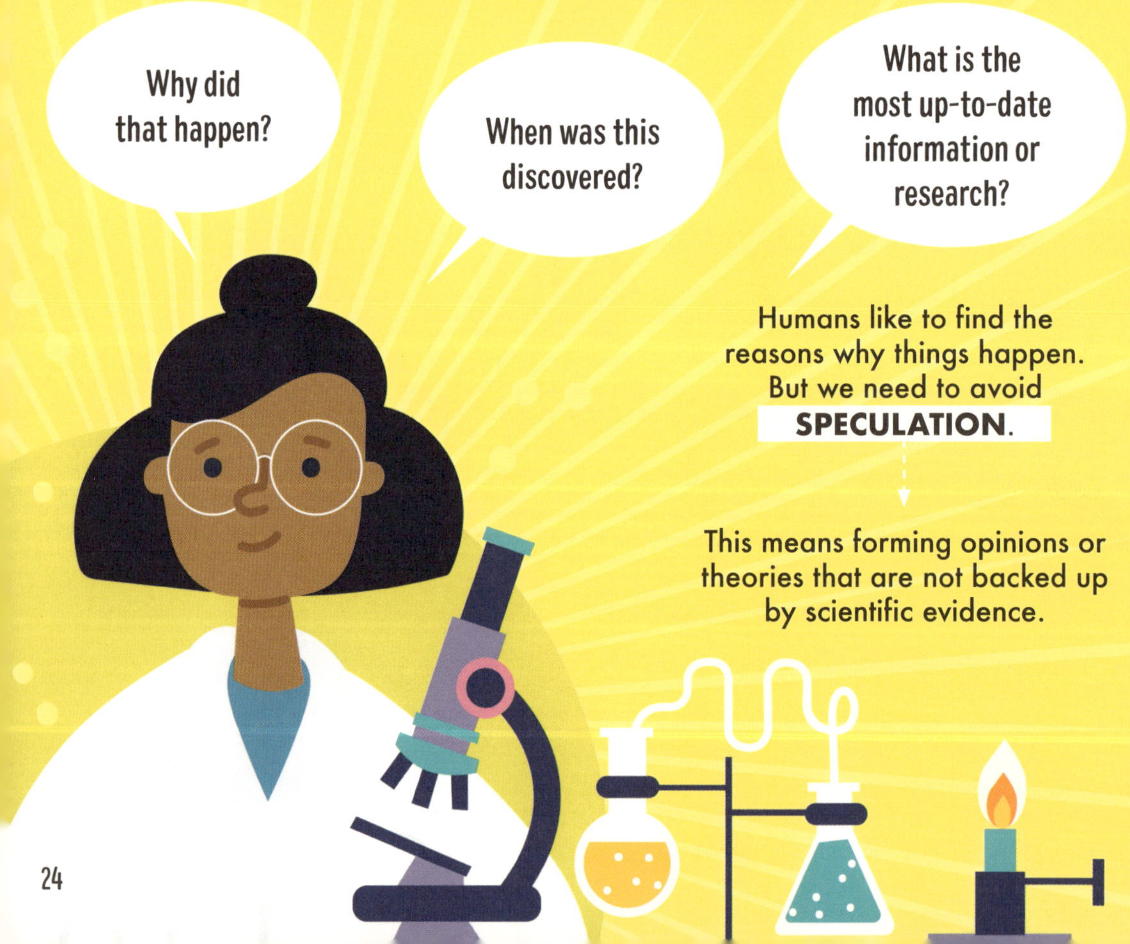

Why did that happen?

When was this discovered?

What is the most up-to-date information or research?

Humans like to find the reasons why things happen. But we need to avoid **SPECULATION**.

This means forming opinions or theories that are not backed up by scientific evidence.

WHAT DO WE KNOW SO FAR ABOUT...

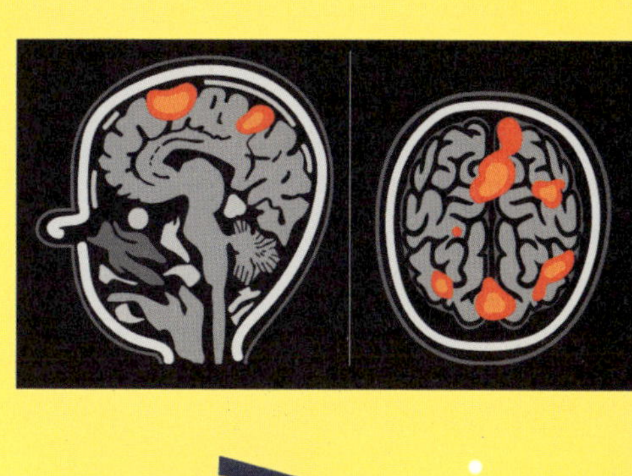

...our incredible brains?

Neuroscientists use technology called fMRI (functional magnetic resonance imaging) scanning to map which bits of our brain we use for different activities. But there is still so much we do not understand about how our brains work—yet!

...the mysterious creatures of the oceans?

More than 80 percent (four-fifths) of our oceans has not been explored, so scientists still do not know how many species exist in the deep. How tragic it would be if we never learn about some of them because climate change wipes them out before we find them.

...the astonishing ecosystems of forests?

Under every forest floor there is a complicated underground network of fungi that connects trees to one another through their roots. Trees can share nutrients through this amazing Wood Wide Web, so it helps to keep the whole forest healthy. Scientists have started to map networks across the world to understand how climate change affects the different fungi and their forests.

ACTIVITY

You could make a timeline of a scientific discovery that inspires you. Find out the most recent facts about it. Maybe there will be future developments too.

WORD TO KNOW

NEUROSCIENTISTS study everything about our brains and nervous systems. The word *neuro* comes from the Greek *neuron*, which means "nerve."

SCIENCE OF THE IMAGINATION

Sometimes the first step to finding out something new in science is to ask some rather mind-boggling questions that stretch our imagination. It's like how your brain feels stronger after you complete a very tricky puzzle or game.

Will humans ever be able to time-travel?
One brilliant theory suggests that wormholes in the universe are like shortcuts through space and time. Anything traveling through a wormhole would move faster than the speed of light and travel through time!

electron

nucleus

proton

neutron

quark

Quarks are found inside protons and neutrons, inside atoms.

What is the smallest particle in the universe?
For now, scientists think the smallest particles are quarks, but this is just what their experiments using the latest equipment have discovered. One day new technology may help us find even tinier ones!

Imaginary worlds
The scientist Albert Einstein did what he called "thought experiments." But this doesn't mean he was trying to become a mind-reader. He imagined experiments that you could never do in real life, like running as fast as a beam of light!

Fiction to fact
In 1983 the science-fiction author Isaac Asimov foresaw the use of robotics in factories and offices. He also predicted that children would learn everything they needed to know from computers. They would still need teachers to inspire them to be curious, though!

Arthur C. Clarke wrote about satellites and communication gadgets he called "personal transceivers" in 1959. This was long before the invention of the mobile phone.

ACTIVITY

Make a time capsule. Write a list of the most up-to-date gadgets you can think of and find some pictures of them. Include your scientific predictions for the future too. Put them in a container with your name and date and hide them at the back of a cupboard. You can look at them in a few years' time. (If you don't forget where the capsule is!)

WORDS TO KNOW

PARTICLES are extremely small pieces of matter. They are the tiny building blocks that make up everything in the universe.

ROBOTICS is the field of technology that involves designing and building machines (**robots**) that make things or do certain repetitive or precise jobs that humans usually do.

WORDS TO KNOW

Analyze means to look at or study something in detail to understand or find out what it means.

Antibiotics are medicines used to treat infections caused by bacteria. They do not work against viruses.

An **antibody** is a substance that our bodies can make. Antibodies travel in our blood and destroy other substances that carry illnesses.

Apparatus is the set of equipment used to do experiments.

A **bacterium** is a tiny, invisible organism. *Bacteria* is the word for more than one. Some bacteria cause diseases. These can be treated with antibiotics.

A **black hole** is a celestial object that forms after a star has exploded. It has such strong gravity that it sucks light into itself and also disturbs the flow of time, making it slow down near the hole.

Carbon dioxide is the gas we breathe out. It is in the atmosphere around us. Normal amounts of it will not harm you.

A **conclusion** is what you decide is true after looking carefully at all the evidence or results.

Consent means agreement or permission to do something.

Data is a collection of facts or information, like measurements, numbers or observations. It is a Latin word, and when used in science, it is plural. You say "The data show."

Eradicate means to get rid of completely.

Estimate means to roughly calculate or judge the extent of something.

Evaluate means to weigh or judge the results of an experiment.

Evidence is anything that helps prove that something is or is not true.

A **formula** is a way of showing or working out how pieces of information like measurements relate to each other. Sometimes **formulae** is used as the plural, but **formulas** is more common.

Gravity is the force that pulls everything on earth toward the center of the planet. Gravity is what gives us weight and makes things fall to the ground.

Hypothesis is an explanation for something that can be tested to see if it is true.

Infographics are a way of showing information using pictures as well as words and numbers.

Misrepresent means to twist information so that people do not get the true facts.

Neuroscientists study everything about our brains and nervous systems. The word *neuro* comes from the Greek *neuron*, which means "nerve."

Particles are extremely small pieces of matter. They are the tiny building blocks that make up everything in the universe.

A **placebo** is a substance that has no medical effect.

Reliable describes information or people you can believe or trust.

Resilient means able to survive difficult conditions or recover quickly after a disaster.

Robotics is the field of technology that involves designing and building machines (robots) that make things or do certain repetitive or precise jobs that humans usually do.

Side effect is an unwanted, sometimes unpleasant, result or symptom.

A **silicon chip** is a tiny piece of silicon inside a computer. It contains electronic circuits and can store lots of information and do complicated calculations.

Speculation is when we or other people come up with opinions or theories that are not backed up by scientific evidence.

Unethical describes someone or something that breaks the proper safe and responsible rules of scientific work.

A **vaccination** is a treatment that gets our own bodies to protect us against diseases.

Validate means to confirm or prove that something is accurate and true.

A **variable** is one thing that is changed during an experiment.

Verify means to check that something is true or correct.

A **virus** is a tiny, invisible organism that is smaller than a bacterium. Viruses cause illnesses like colds, chicken pox and COVID-19. These cannot be treated with antibiotic medicines.

ANSWERS TO ACTIVITIES

page 3
An egg is denser than unsalted water, so it does not float. Adding salt to water makes it denser than the egg. Therefore, an egg will float in salt water.

pages 8–9 1.B; 2.D; 3.A; 4.E; 5.C.

page 15

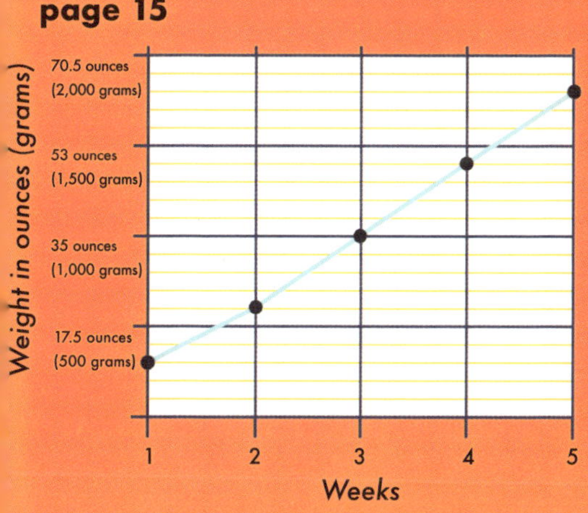

pages 16–17
The speed of the bicycle is 6.25 miles (10 kilometers) per hour.

page 23
Your Breakfast's Journey:
Mouth → stomach → small intestine → large intestine → anus (as poop!)

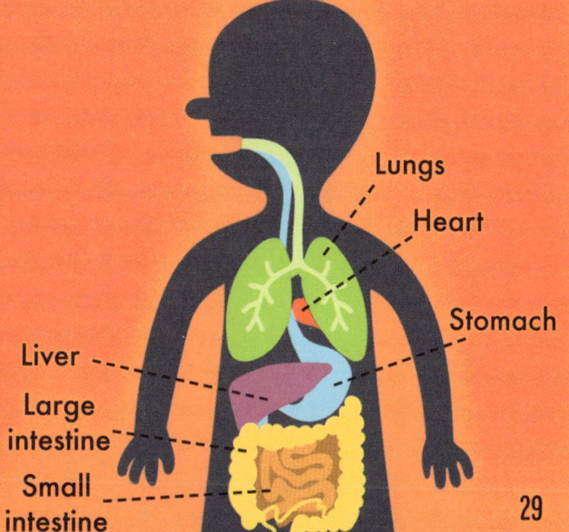

BE A SCIENTIST!

What kind of scientist would you like to be? Perhaps you want to help the environment or explore the oceans. Maybe you would like to investigate black holes, invent a new material or discover more about our brilliant brains.

Safe science at home

You could start being a scientist now!

- Plan and design your experiment carefully. (Check with an adult before you start.)
- Make sure your experiment is a fair test (see page 3), and record your results clearly.
- Analyze the data. What conclusions can you make from the information?
- Remember that scientists **never stop asking questions!** (You can also use big scientific words because you know what they mean now.)

SCIENTIFIC FACT-FINDING
How do you check the science behind your experiments or the facts about a science story you have read online or in the news?

RESEARCH
information using reliable sources like...

The **encyclopedia** and up-to-date books written by specialists.

Websites of academic institutions like universities, specialist organizations like NOAA, Environment Canada, the National Weather Service, NASA, museums and research stations.

Some of these sources post information on social media, but be sure to check first that anything you read is actually from one of these reliable sources.

REMEMBER...

WHO
are the scientists behind the information?

CHECK
the dates of the information to make sure you are getting the most up-to-date facts.

CORROBORATE
the facts by looking at more than one source of information.

SUSAN MARTINEAU is an author, editor and first-class fact finder who writes creative and educational books for children. Her book *Real-Life Mysteries* was the winner of the Blue Peter Book Award for Best Book with Facts 2018. She has been writing information books for children for over 20 years, but began her career as a nonfiction-books editor with the BBC in London. She has lived in several different countries, including France and Malaysia, but is now based back in the UK. She was a kid who always wanted to know about everything, so she researches and writes the kind of books she would have liked as a child!

VICKY BARKER is b small publishing's creative director and a Blue Peter Book Award–winning illustrator for *Real-Life Mysteries*. Vicky graduated from Liverpool John Moores University and has designed and illustrated for publishers such as Usborne, Egmont and Catnip. For b small publishing, Vicky has illustrated the STEM Starters for Kids series, *Paper Toys*, *Infographics for Kids*, *FACTS*, *Geographics* and many more. Vicky lives by the sea in West Sussex.

INDEX